D1116665

Totally AMAZING FACTS ABOUT MILITARY SEA and AIR VEHICLES

CARI MEISTER

CAPSTONE PRESS
a capstone imprint

The C-130 can carry more than **40,000 POUNDS** (18,142 kilograms) of supplies!

It can airdrop **TANKS** from its rear.

KEIKO, the orca from *Free Willy,* was flown to the movie set in a C-130.

U.S. AIR FORCE

YJ
AF 74 685

3

The **inflatoplane** was designed in the **1950s** to be **airdropped** to pilots stuck behind enemy lines.

The plane could be inflated in **FIVE** minutes!

WHEN COMPACTED, IT COULD FIT IN A WHEELBARROW.

The Fokker DR.1 was a TRI-PLANE: it had THREE wings!

No original Fokkers exist today. Only copies do.

THE RED BARON, THE MOST FEARED PILOT OF WORLD WAR I (1914-1918), FLEW A FOKKER.

The B-52 can drop or launch a wider variety of weapons than any other U.S. aircraft.

The B-52 has been in use since the 1940S.

THE B-1B CARRIES MORE GUIDED AND UNGUIDED WEAPONS THAN ANY OTHER U.S. MILITARY PLANE.

It can track, target, and engage moving vehicles in split seconds.

At sea level, the B-1B can fly

MACH 1.2!

That's almost twice the speed that a passenger jet flies.

THE HARRIER IS THE ONLY FIGHTER JET THAT CAN TAKE OFF AND LAND VERTICALLY.

THE JET CAN FLY MORE THAN 630 MILES PER HOUR (1,010 kilometers per hour)!

Its MASSIVE turbofan engines are made by ROLLS-ROYCE.

The VALKYRIE BOMBER could fly MACH 3!

That's more than twice as fast as the B1-B bomber.

The plane was built to be a **LONG-RANGE NUCLEAR BOMBER,** but was never used for that purpose.

ONLY TWO VALKYRIE BOMBERS WERE EVER PRODUCED. ONLY ONE SURVIVES TODAY.

The British used **BLIMPS** as navy patrol ships.

They were used to spot and fire at German subs.

16

PARACHUTES WERE RARELY CARRIED ON AIRSHIP FLIGHTS AT THE BEGINNING OF THE WAR.

THEY WERE DEEMED UNNECESSARY.

ALMOST 6,000 BEAUFIGHTERS WERE BUILT BETWEEN 1940 AND 1946.

THE BEAU WAS CALLED "WHISPERING DEATH" BY THE JAPANESE BECAUSE THE ENGINES WERE SO QUIET.

Its quiet ENGINES and RADAR SYSTEM made this plane a stealthy nighttime fighter.

The **KIOWA** was the first army helicopter to have an all-glass cockpit.

KIOWAS can be armed with HELLFIRE MISSILES, HYDRA 70 ROCKETS, STRINGER MISSILES, OR MACHINE GUNS.

THE OH-1 IS QUICK AND STEALTHY.

Its nickname is "THE NINJA."

It can fly 168 miles per hour (270 kph)!

IT HAS TANDEM, OR SIDE-BY-SIDE, COCKPITS.

The ORION is considered the TOP maritime patrolling airplane in the world.

IT IS RESPONSIBLE FOR KEEPING OCEAN WATERS SAFE FROM ENEMIES.

It is used by **17** different countries and has a 16-HOUR nonstop flytime.

THE PLANE IS SOMETIMES USED TO FIND MODERN DAY PIRATES.

LET'S COMPARE:

SOPWITH CAMEL

COUNTRY: United Kingdom

YEAR MADE: 1917

NO. OF WINGS: 2

SPEED (MPH/KPH): 115/185

WEAPONS: 2 Vickers machine guns

RATE OF CLIMB: 1,085 feet (331 meters) per minute

WWI FIGHTER PLANES

VS. THE FOKKER D.VII

Germany

1918

2

117/188

2 Spandau machine guns

772 feet (235 meters) per minute

LET'S COMPARE:

EARLY ATTACK HELICOPTER WITH FUTURE ATTACK HELICOPTER

COUNTRY:

YEAR IN SERVICE:

MAXIMUM SPEED (MPH/KPH):

MAXIMUM RANGE (MI/KM):

WEAPONS:

MIL-MI 24 (HIND)

Soviet Union

1973

208/335

99/159

machine guns/
rockets/missiles

SIKORSKY S-97 RAIDER

United States

2020

253/407

354/570

machine guns/
cannons/missiles

The T-50 is a large FIGHTER.

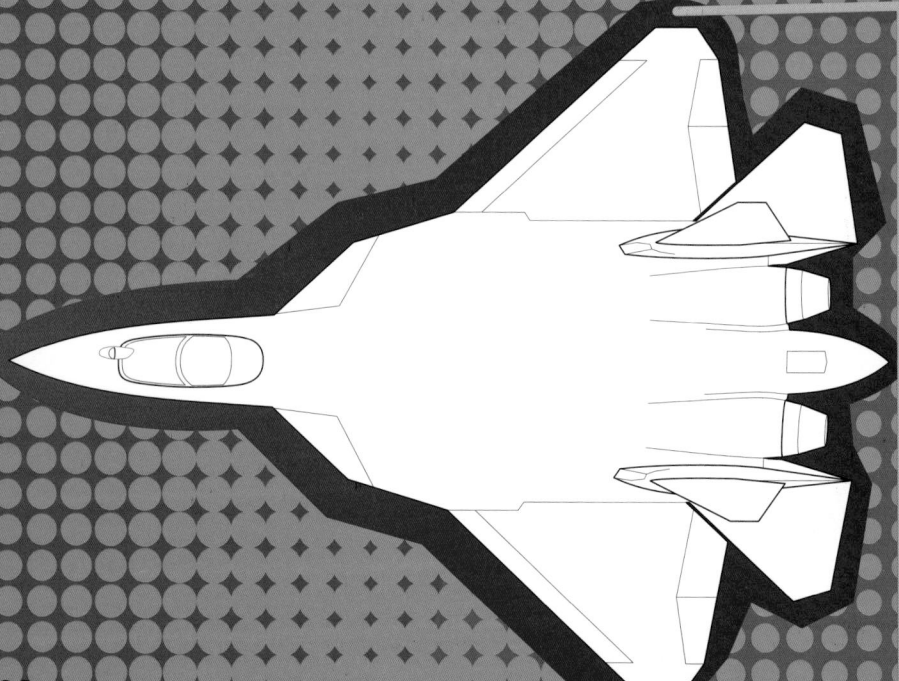

Its wingspan is about 50 FEET (15 M)!

It can reach **MACH 4** in just a few seconds.

That's over **3,000** miles per hour (4,830 kph)!

IT CARRIES ADVANCED X-74M2 CRUISE MISSILES.

THE F-15 IS A REMARKABLE AIRCRAFT IN EVERY WAY.

IT CAN LAND SAFELY WITH ONLY ONE WING!

IT HAS A PERFECT RECORD: ZERO AIR COMBAT LOSSES.

The F-15 can successfully shoot down satellites.

The B-2 is covered with a special paint that makes it almost invisible to ground-based sensors.

34

In 2003 JENNIFER WILSON became the first female pilot to fly the B-2 in a COMBAT MISSION.

ONE B-2 COSTS ABOUT $1.2 BILLION.

The Mustang was considered the BEST FIGHTER of WORLD WAR II (1939–1945)

413926

E2 S

because it could fly farther and faster than most of the other aircraft of the day.

MORE THAN 15,000 MUSTANGS WERE MADE.

Pilots from at least 25 DIFFERENT countries flew the Mustang.

DURING WORLD WAR II, MUSTANG PILOTS SHOT DOWN ALMOST 5,000 ENEMY AIRCRAFT.

The AEROCYCLE was designed in the 1950s to be a "FLYING PLATFORM."

A PILOT COULD STEER IT BY SIMPLY SHIFTING HIS WEIGHT.

THE PROJECT WAS CANCELED AFTER THERE WERE TOO MANY TESTING CRASHES.

The ANTONOV AN-225 is the world's LARGEST MILITARY TRANSPORT AIRPLANE.

IT WAS BIG ENOUGH TO CARRY THE ROCKET BOOSTERS FOR THE SOVIET SPACE SHUTTLE.

IT IS 276 FEET (84 M) LONG.

That's longer than approximately five sperm whales lined up end to end!

The C-5 is America's largest WORKING CARGO AIRPLANE.

U.S. AIR FORCE

The paint alone weighs 2,600 pounds (1,179 kg)!

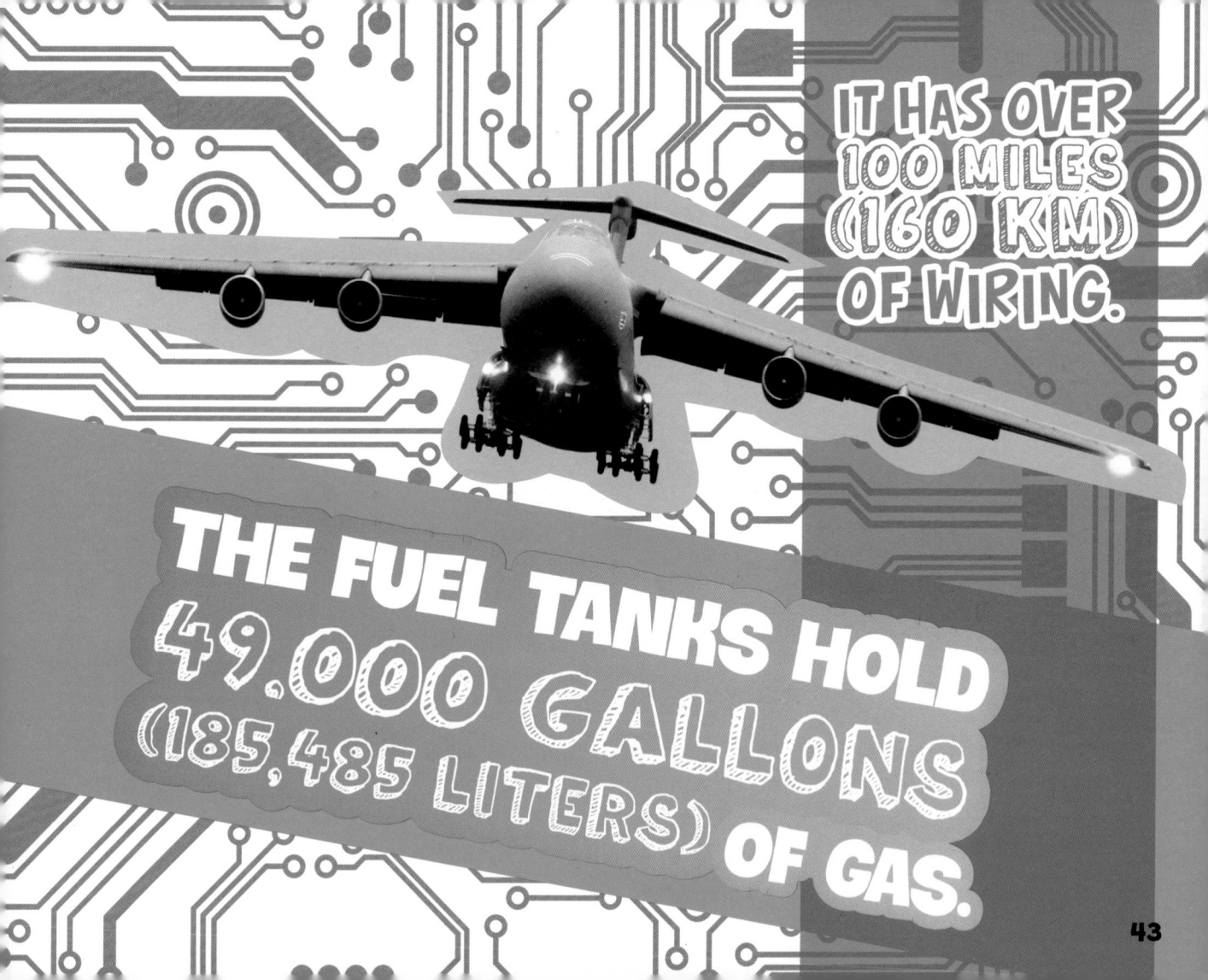

IT HAS OVER 100 MILES (160 KM) OF WIRING.

THE FUEL TANKS HOLD 49,000 GALLONS (185,485 LITERS) OF GAS.

CHINOOKS
are very rarely retired. They are fixed instead.

The CH-47D model can lift 19,500 POUNDS (8,845 KG)!

One pilot who fought in AFGHANISTAN (2001–2014) flew the exact same CHINOOK his grandfather flew more than 50 YEARS earlier in the VIETNAM WAR (1955–1975).

The VOUGHT V-173 was dubbed the "FLYING PANCAKE" for obvious reasons!

WHEN PEOPLE SAW THE V-173 FLYING, THEY THOUGHT IT WAS A UFO.

It was almost the first vertical-lifting aircraft to go into production. But it was scrapped due to funding issues.

The HERON is an aircraft PILOTED BY REMOTE CONTROL.

48

IT IS USED FOR SPYING, SO IT DOESN'T CARRY ANY WEAPONS.

IT CAN FLY FOR **24 HOURS** AT A TIME.

The media called this aircraft "A MAMMOTH WATER SPIDER."

IT NEVER LEFT THE TESTING STAGES BECAUSE IT HAD TOO MANY UNRESOLVED PROBLEMS.

50

THE PILOT WHO FLEW IT SAID, "THE FLIGHT WAS LIKE RIDING A **POGO STICK** IN A SITTING POSITION— up, down, up, down."

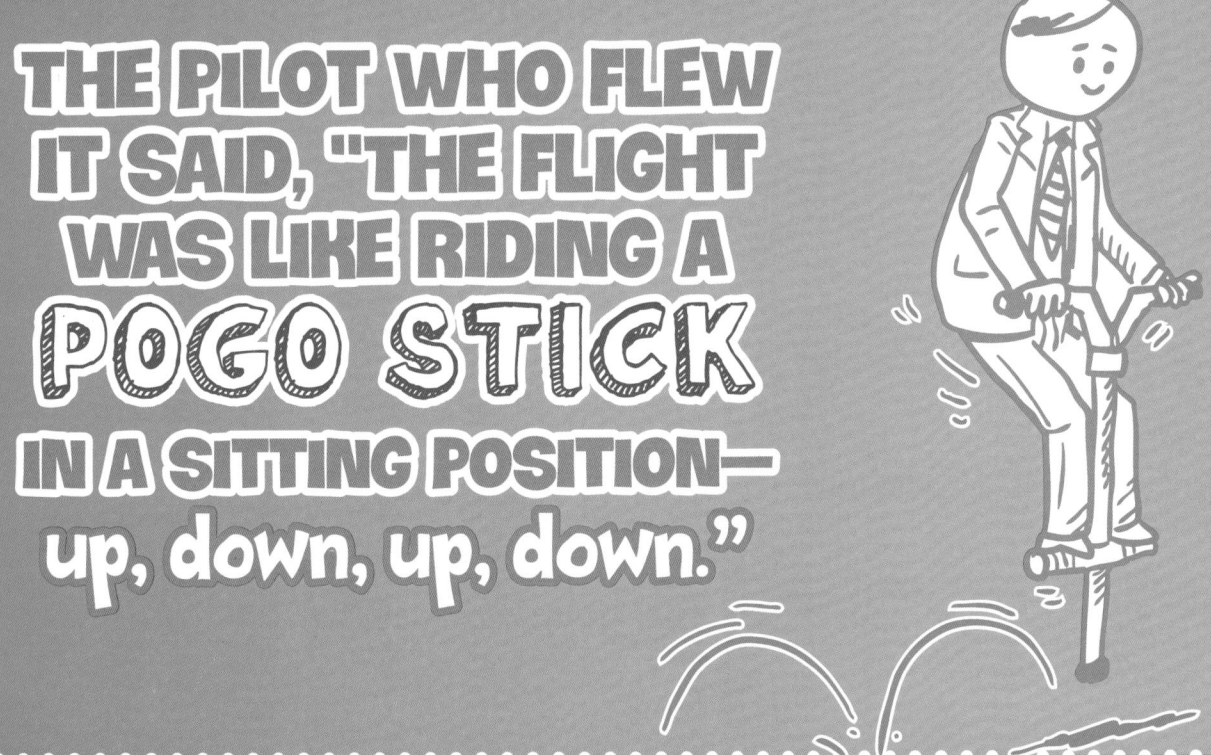

The rotors were almost 130 feet (40 m) long! That's about as long as 16 horses all lined up.

SUKHOI T-50 STEALTH FIGHTER

F-15CJ/DJ

F-22A

SU-30MKV

SU-27SK

F-15K

 UNITED STATES

 CHINA

 SOUTH KOREA

 JAPAN

 VIETNAM

 RUSSIA

The ATLANT will be ready in **2018** and will combine HOVERCRAFT, AIRPLANE, HELICOPTER, and AIRSHIP TECHNOLOGY into one vehicle.

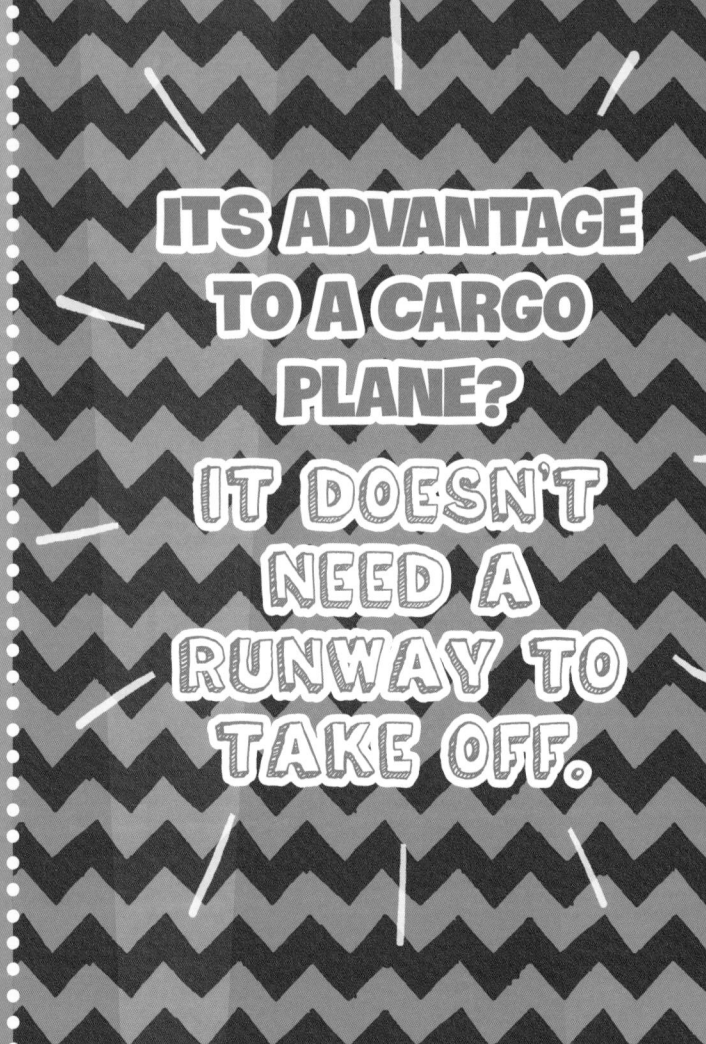

ITS ADVANTAGE TO A CARGO PLANE?

IT DOESN'T NEED A RUNWAY TO TAKE OFF.

IT CAN LAND OR TAKE OFF FROM ANYWHERE.

THIS AIRCRAFT, TESTED IN 1957–1960, WAS DUBBED "The Flying Jeep."

The pilot sat in the open air in a seat at the front of the aircraft.

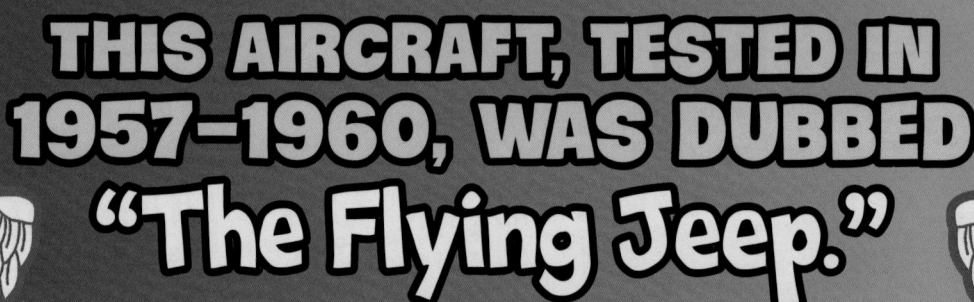

IT TOPPED OUT AT 32 MILES PER HOUR (51 KPH).

THE FLYING JEEP WAS VERY EASY TO FLY, BUT IT COULDN'T GO HIGH ENOUGH. SO THE ARMY SCRAPPED IT.

This fighter jet didn't need a runway.

IT USED THE OCEAN!

IT HAD HYDRO-SKIS FOR TAKEOFF AND LANDING.

SEA DART WAS THE **FIRST** AND **ONLY** SEAPLANE TO EVER REACH SUPERSONIC SPEEDS.

SADLY, DURING ONE OF ITS TEST FLIGHTS, IT disintegrated. THE SEA DART WAS NEVER USED IN SERVICE.

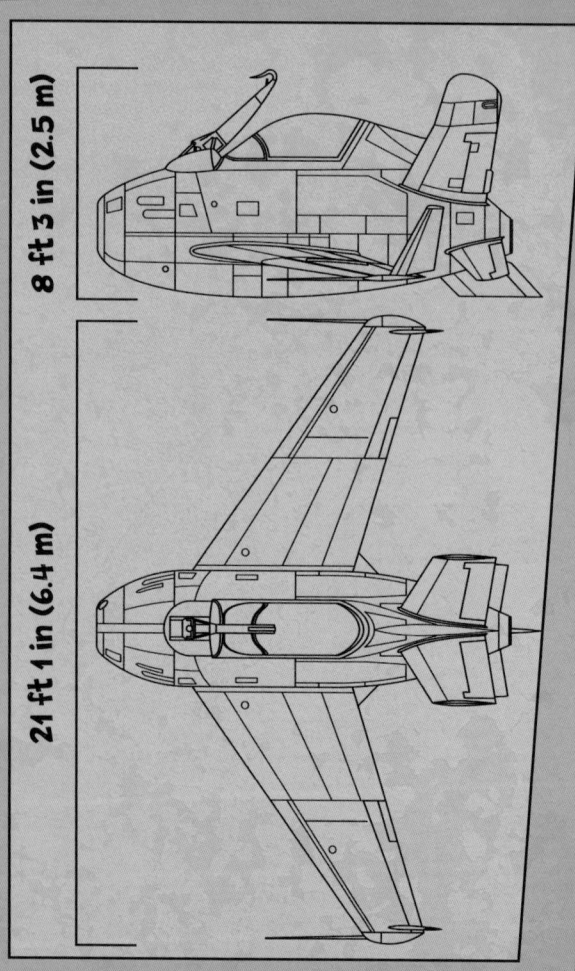

8 ft 3 in (2.5 m)

21 ft 1 in (6.4 m)

THE GOBLIN IS THE SMALLEST JET-PROPELLED FIGHTER EVER BUILT.

IT WAS MADE TO BE CARRIED AND LAUNCHED FROM A B-36 BOMBER.

The Goblin flew fine.
But it had other problems,
so it was cancelled.

Leduc 010 Ramjet (France)

THE LEDUC 010 RAMJET
RODE PIGGYBACK ON
ANOTHER PLANE
FOR ITS FIRST FEW FLIGHTS.

After that, the Leduc 010 was the first aircraft to fly using only ramjet power.

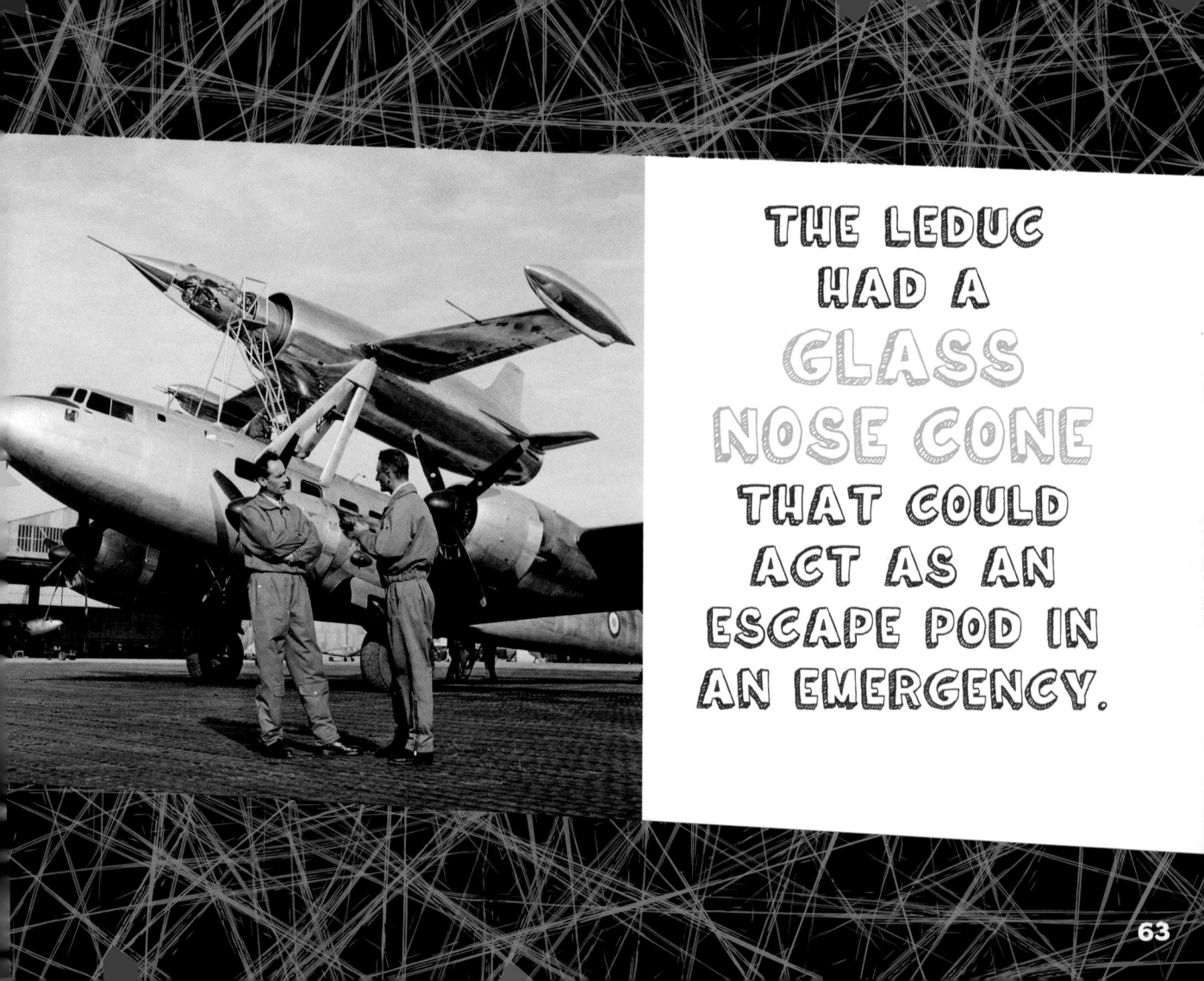

THE LEDUC
HAD A
GLASS
NOSE CONE
THAT COULD
ACT AS AN
ESCAPE POD IN
AN EMERGENCY.

63

German U-Boats (Germany)

During World War II, 430 civilian and Allied ships were sunk by U-boats.

U-BOATS WERE VERY COMPLICATED: THERE WERE AROUND 50 HANDWHEELS INSIDE USED TO MANAGE PRESSURE.

Most U-boats had emblems. The U-47's was a snorting bull.

...The Story of the Doomed U-1206

The U-1206 started its first patrol in April of **1945.**

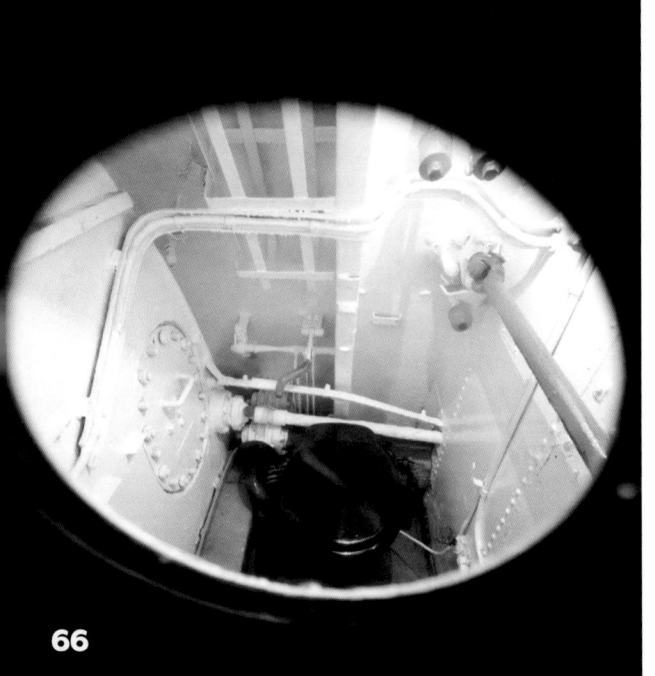

ON **APRIL 14,** THE COMMANDER WAS FORCED TO SURFACE THE SUB BECAUSE OF A **MALFUNCTIONING TOILET.**

THE SUB WAS IMMEDIATELY BOMBED BY A BRITISH SHIP.

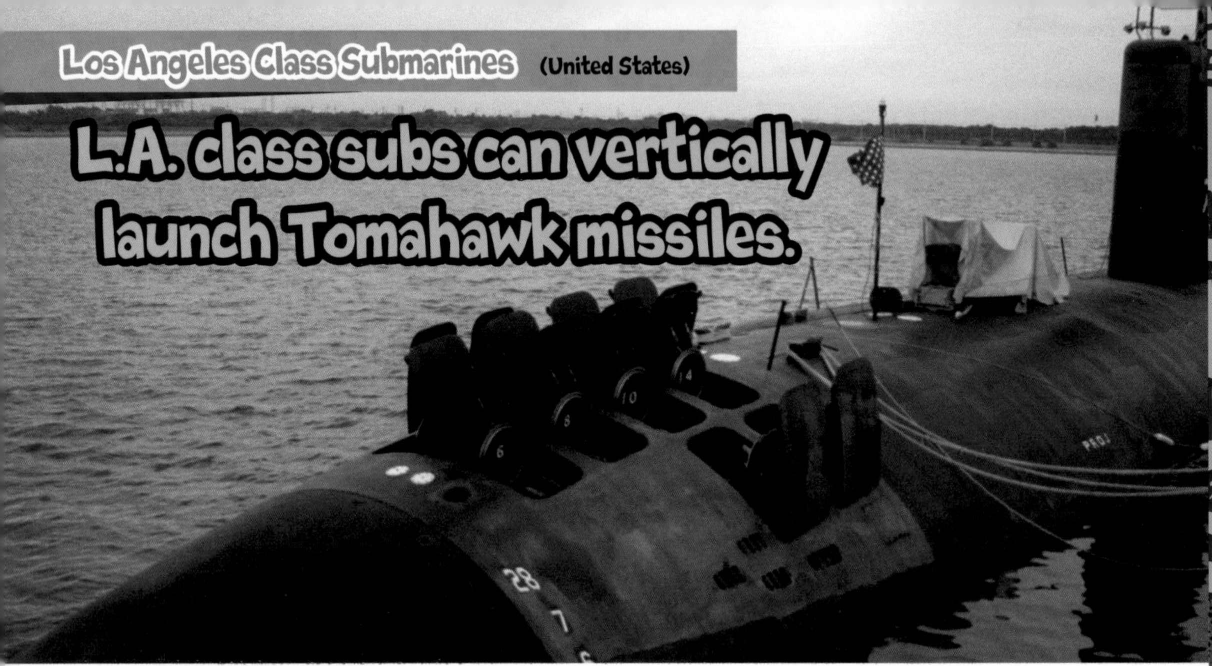

L.A. class subs can vertically launch Tomahawk missiles.

THESE SUBS ARE PROPELLED BY NUCLEAR REACTORS.

ONE SUB COSTS ABOUT $900 MILLION DOLLARS TO BUILD.

L.A. CLASS SUBS WEIGH 6,900 TONS EACH!

69

BEFORE A SUBMARINE CAN DIVE, THE CREW HAS TO PERFORM MORE THAN

225

OPERATIONAL CHECKS.

TUBE EMPTY

SUBS ARE PAINTED BLACK SO THEY CAN HIDE UNDERWATER FROM ENEMIES.

SUBS CAN DIVE MORE THAN **800 FEET (245 M).** BUT EXACTLY HOW DEEP A SUB CAN DIVE IS CLASSIFIED INFORMATION.

IN 1921 THE R-14 SUB RAN OUT OF FUEL WHILE AT SEA.

The sailors made sails out of blankets, curtain rods, and hammocks.

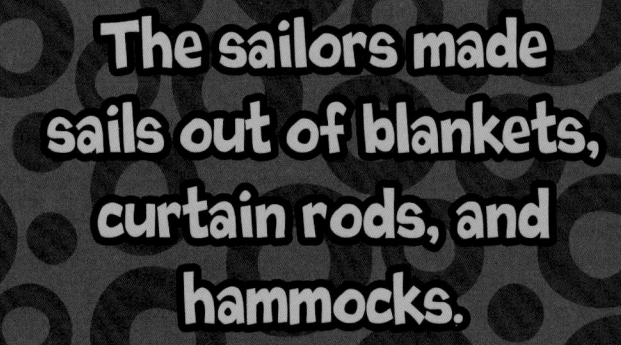

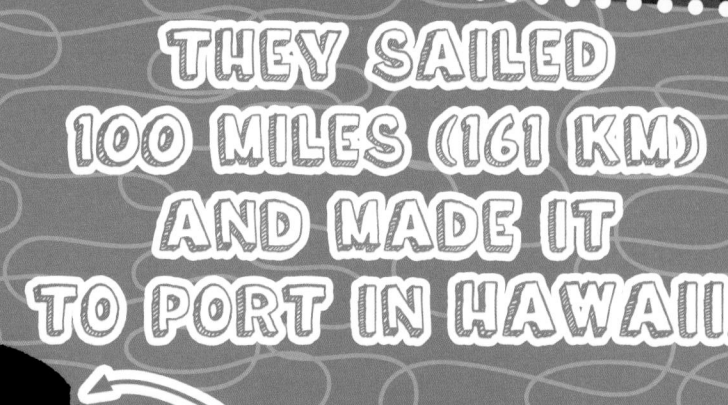

HAWAII

THEY SAILED 100 MILES (161 KM) AND MADE IT TO PORT IN HAWAII.

THE USS *NEW YORK'S* BOW WAS MADE WITH 7.5 TONS OF STEEL FROM THE FALLEN WORLD TRADE CENTER BUILDINGS.

The ship's motto is : "Strength forged through sacrifice. Never forget."

IT IS THE ONLY NAVY SHIP THAT HAS EIGHT-SIDED MASTS.

Advanced enclosed masts

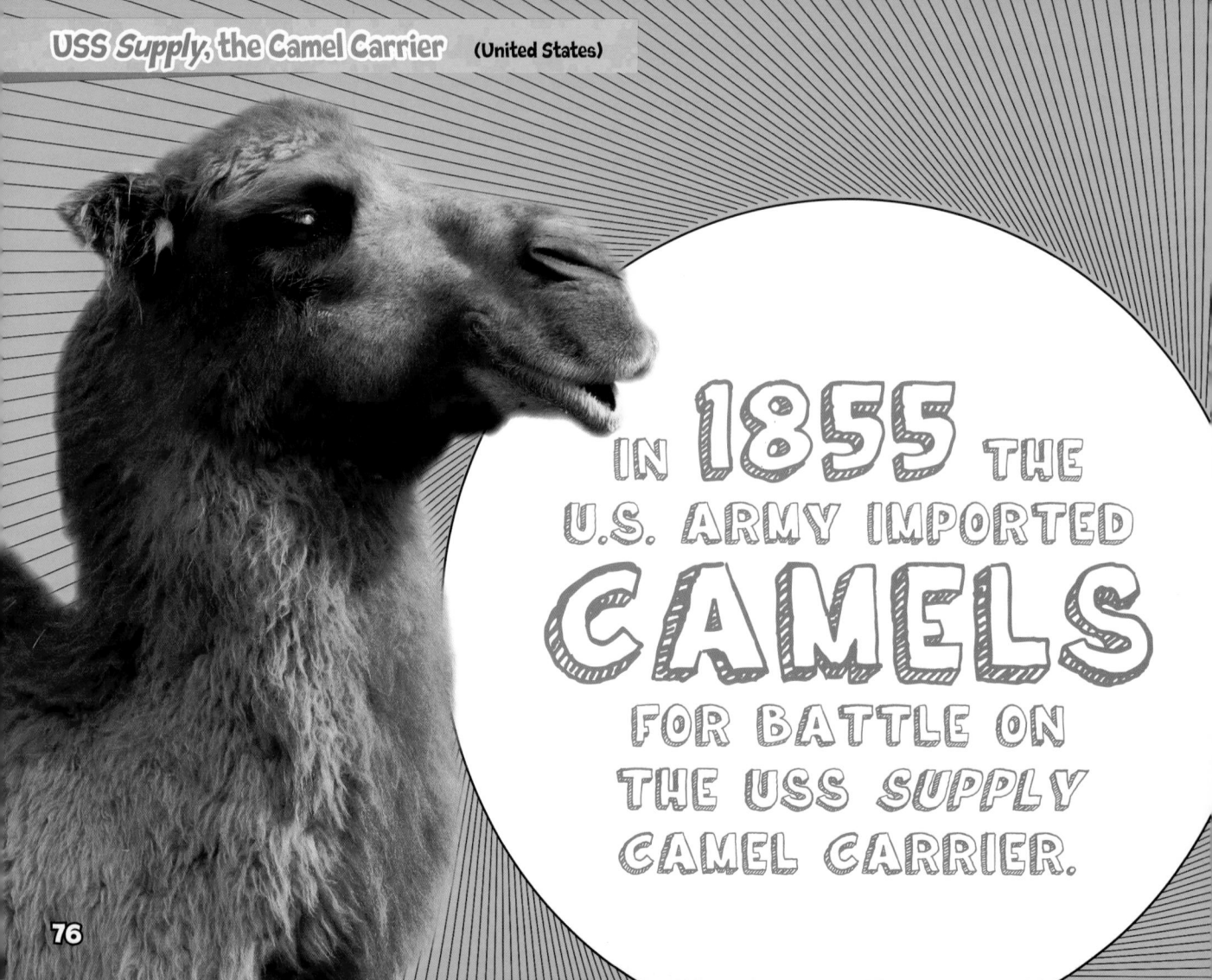

IN 1855 THE U.S. ARMY IMPORTED CAMELS FOR BATTLE ON THE USS *SUPPLY* CAMEL CARRIER.

TO FIT THE CAMELS AND THEIR LARGE HUMPS, WORKERS CUT AWAY PART OF THE **SHIP'S MAIN DECK.**

THE CAMELS MADE IT TO THE UNITED STATES BUT WERE NEVER USED FOR BATTLE.

IN 1945 THE U.S. NAVY USED A REFRIGERATED BARGE TO DELIVER ICE CREAM TO NAVY SHIPS.

THE BARGE COULD MAKE 10 GALLONS (38 LITERS) OF ICE CREAM EVERY SEVEN MINUTES.

The barge went from ship to ship all over the Pacific Ocean.

Lun-class Ekranoplan (Russian/Soviet)

Is it a BOAT or a PLANE?

THE LUN WAS A MASSIVE GROUND EFFECT VEHICLE (GEV) WITH A 148-FOOT (45-METER) WINGSPAN.

80

IT USED THE AIR CURRENTS MADE BY ITS HUGE WINGS TO "FLY" ABOVE THE WATER'S SURFACE.

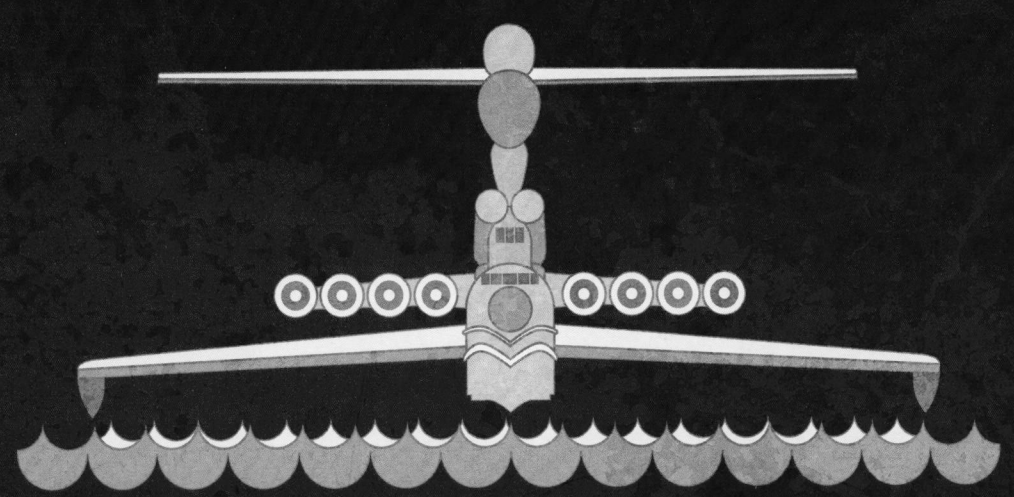

THE LUN HAD ONLY A LARGE HYDRO-SKI FOR LANDING.

SWCS STANDS FOR "SHALLOW WATER COMBAT SUBMERSIBLE."

THESE ARE "MINI-SUBS" FOR NAVY SEALS, A SPECIAL FORCES UNIT IN THE U.S. NAVY.

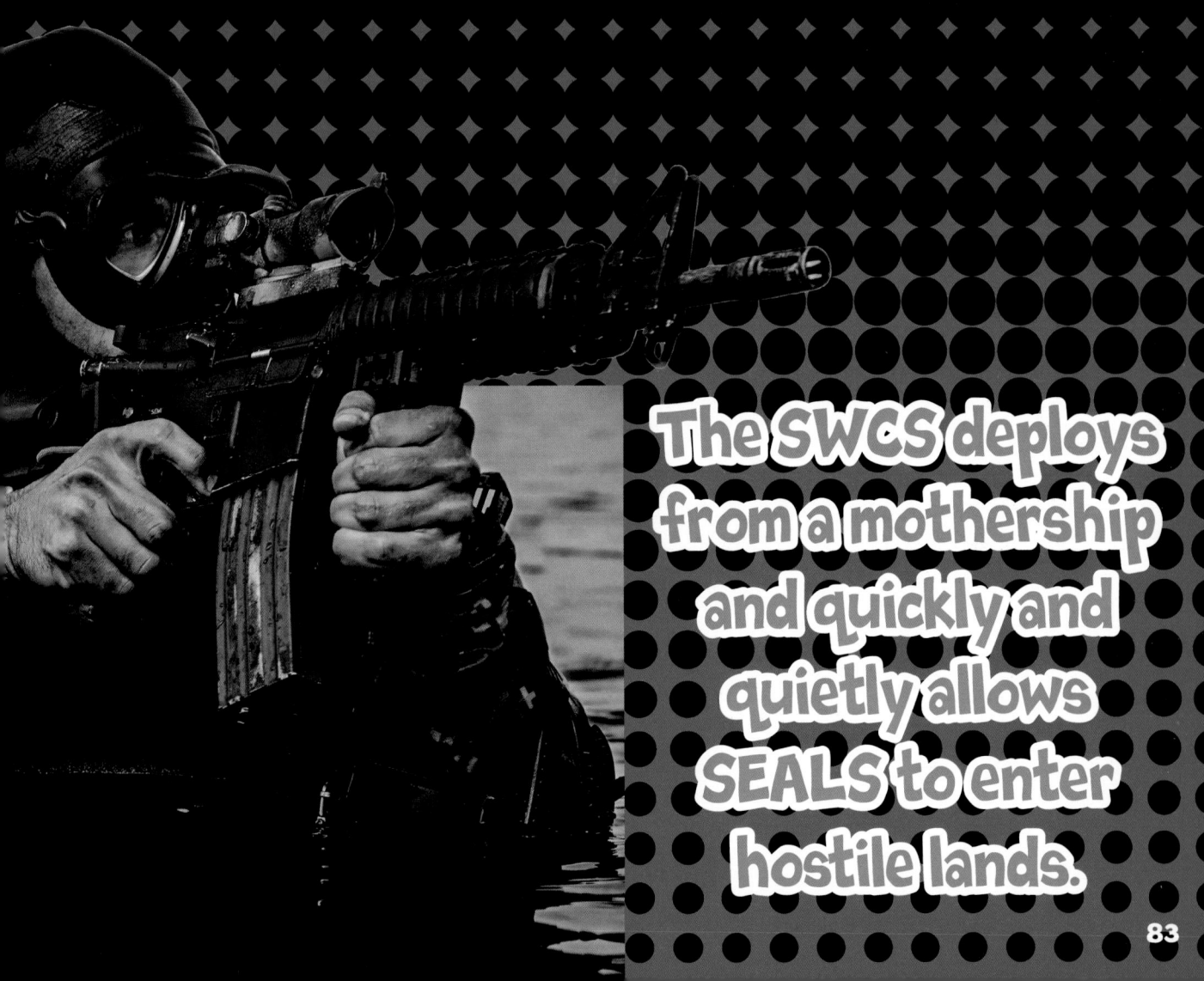

The SWCS deploys from a mothership and quickly and quietly allows SEALS to enter hostile lands.

The LCS is the U.S. Navy's newest class of warship.

Although the ships are small, they can go **40 KNOTS (46 MPH/74 KPH)!**

COMMANDER JOHN KOCHENDORFER CALLS IT, "THE COOLEST SHIP OUT THERE. A MILITARY JET SKI WITH A FLIGHT DECK AND A GUN."

The
USS VESUVIUS

served in the Spanish-American War (1898).
It was the only ship to use guns that shot

DYNAMITE.

ITS ONE **MAJOR FLAW** WAS THAT ITS GUNS WERE NOT ON SWIVELS. IF A SOLDIER WANTED TO REDIRECT A GUN'S AIM, THE **WHOLE SHIP** HAD TO MOVE.

ONLY **ONE** IX-529 WAS EVER BUILT. IT WAS THE WORLD'S FIRST **STEALTH SHIP**.

THE U.S. MILITARY NEVER REALLY USED THE *SEA SHADOW.* SO THEY SOLD IT FOR SCRAP IN 2012.

The ship in the James Bond movie *Tomorrow Never Dies* was based on the *Sea Shadow.*

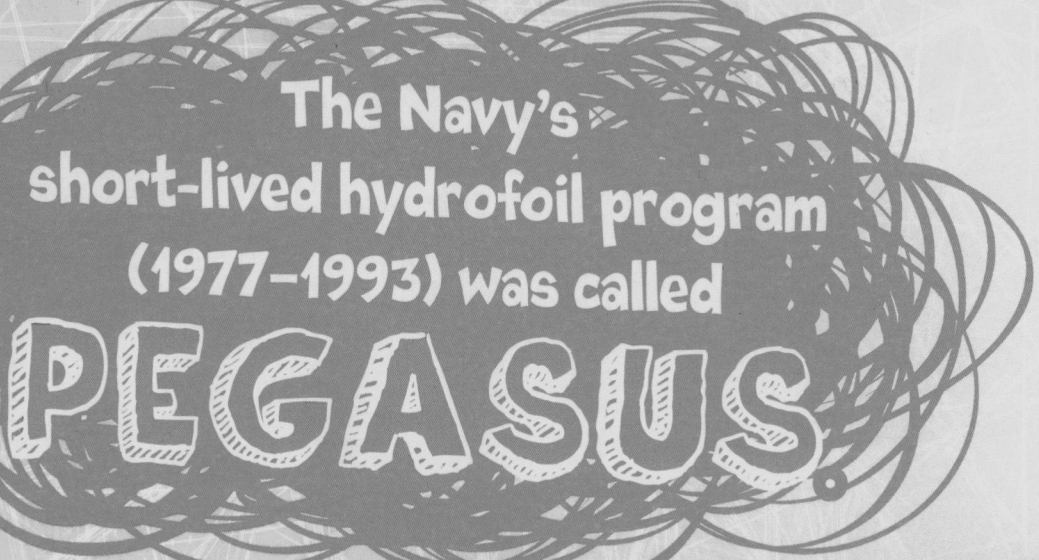

The Navy's short-lived hydrofoil program (1977–1993) was called

PEGASUS

WHEN "FOILBORNE" THE SHIP COULD GO MORE THAN 48 KNOTS (55 MPH/90 KPH)!

TO GO "FOILBORNE" THE SHIP'S **HYDROFOILS** (winglike structures) WOULD LIFT THE SHIPS INTO THE **AIR**.

DURING WORLD WAR II, THE BRITISH WANTED TO BUILD AN AIRCRAFT CARRIER WITH **ICE** AND **WOOD PULP**.

They made a model that was 30 feet (9 m) wide by 60 feet (18 m) long to test its **strength**.

THE MODEL WAS **DURABLE.** BUT FUNDING ISSUES CAUSED THE PROJECT TO **FAIL.**

THE FS *MARJATA* IS ONE OF THE WORLD'S TOP SPY SHIPS —AND IT'S SHAPED LIKE A PIZZA SLICE!

RUSSIA

Its main job is to spy on the Russian military in the Arctic Sea.

IT'S SO SOPHISTICATED THAT NOT MANY PEOPLE REALLY KNOW EVERYTHING IT CAN DO.

WE DO KNOW THAT IT HAS THE MOST HIGH-TECH SPY GEAR AROUND.

THE MOST POWERFUL ICEBREAKER IS CURRENTLY BEING BUILT IN RUSSIA.

It will be able to break through ice that's 9.8 feet (3 m) thick!

ICEBREAKERS GLIDE ONTO ICE AND THEN USE THEIR WEIGHT TO BREAK THROUGH IT.

LET'S COMPARE:

BNS BARROSO

COUNTRY: Brazil

YEAR IN SERVICE: 2008

SURFACE SPEED: 27 knots

RANGE: 4,063 miles (6,539 km)

WEAPONS: missiles, guns, torpedoes

NAVAL CORVETTE WARSHIPS

VS.

CNS BENGBU

China

2013

28 knots

2,300 miles (3,701 km)

missiles, guns, torpedoes

LET'S COMPARE:

LENGTHS OF NAVY SHIPS

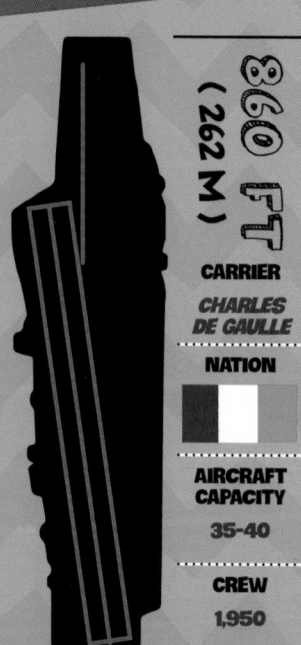

860 FT (262 M)

CARRIER

CHARLES DE GAULLE

NATION

AIRCRAFT CAPACITY

35-40

CREW

1,950

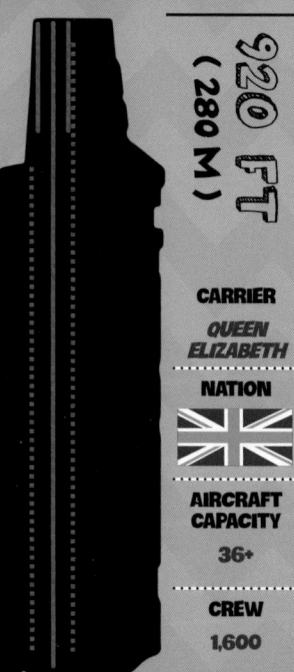

920 FT (280 M)

CARRIER

QUEEN ELIZABETH

NATION

AIRCRAFT CAPACITY

36+

CREW

1,600

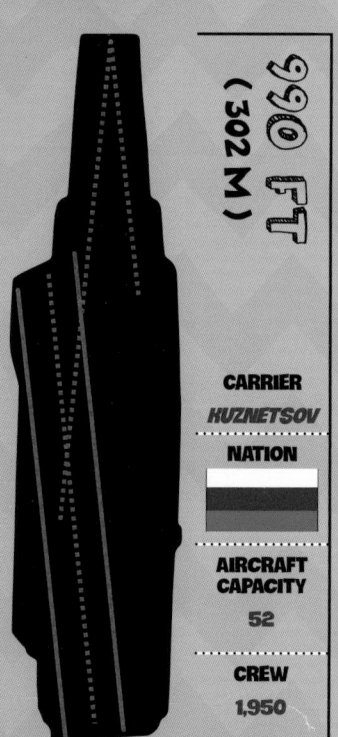

990 FT
(302 M)

CARRIER

KUZNETSOV

NATION

AIRCRAFT
CAPACITY

52

CREW

1,950

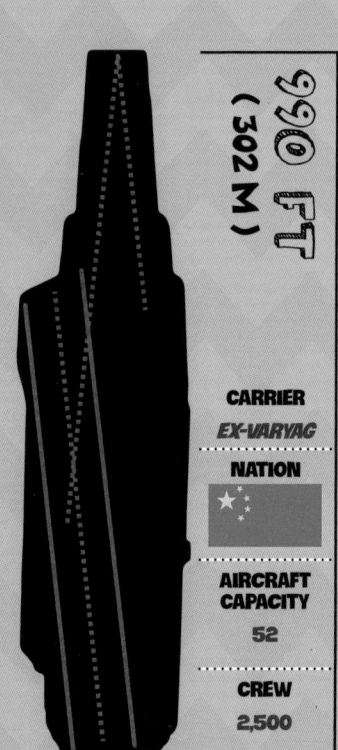

990 FT
(302 M)

CARRIER

EX-VARYAG

NATION

AIRCRAFT
CAPACITY

52

CREW

2,500

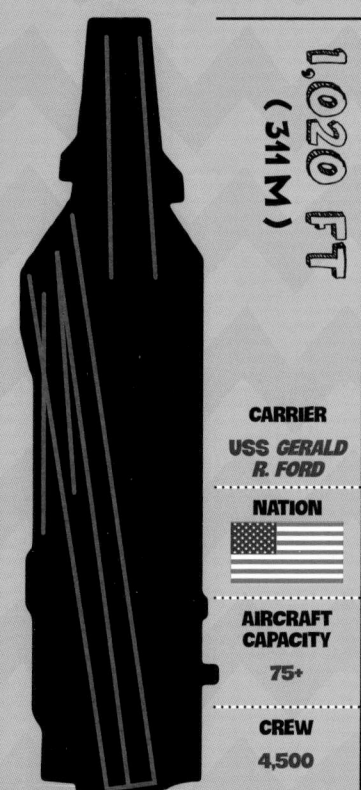

1,020 FT
(311 M)

CARRIER

USS *GERALD
R. FORD*

NATION

AIRCRAFT
CAPACITY

75+

CREW

4,500

LET'S COMPARE:

INDIA'S FLEET

NATO Class	Engine Type	Fleet Size	Speed	Crew Size		
Chakra	☢	1	28-35 knots	73	131 yards (120 m)	
Sindhughosh	🔴	9	20 knots	52-68	82 yards (75 m)	
Shishumar	🔴	4	22.5 knots	73	66 yards (60 m)	

☢ Nuclear   🔴 Diesel

INDIAN AND CHINESE SUBS

CHINA'S FLEET

NATO Class	Engine Type	Fleet Size	Speed	Crew Size		
Jin	☢	3	>20 knots	120	153 yards (140 m)	
Xia	☢	1	22 knots	140	131 yards (120 m)	
Shang	☢	2	30 knots	100	120 yards (110 m)	

HOVERCRAFTS RIDE ON A CUSHION OF AIR AND ARE MADE TO LAND TROOPS ON BEACHES.

Russia and Ukraine have the largest military hovercrafts. Each one can carry **THREE BATTLE TANKS!**

AT HIGH SPEEDS, MODERN HOVERCRAFTS LEAVE ALMOST NO WAKE.

HOSPITAL SHIPS
are giant moving
HOSPITALS.

U.S. NAVAL HOSPITAL SHIP
COMFORT

MILITARY HOSPITAL SHIPS HELP INJURED SOLDIERS. BUT THEY ALSO HELP PEOPLE ALL OVER THE WORLD IN NEED OF MEDICAL CARE.

THE USNS MERCY IS THE LENGTH OF THREE FOOTBALL FIELDS AND CONTAINS 1,000 BEDS.

U.S. NAVY SHIP LINGO

If you are on a Navy ship there are a few words you need to know:

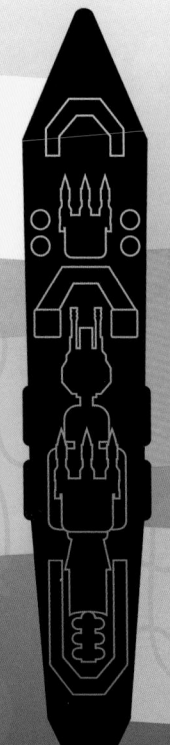

BOW
the front of the ship

PORT
facing forward, the left-hand side of a ship

STARBOARD
facing forward, the right-hand side of a ship

STERN
the back of the ship

Some other terms:

MESS DECK
where you eat food

DECK
a level where you walk on the ship

THE RACK
where you sleep

THE HEAD
where you would find a toilet.

BULKHEADS
walls

GLOSSARY

airships—a large aircraft that does not have wings but has a body filled with gas (like helium or hydrogen) so that it floats

assault vehicles—armed vehicles that are used to attack or defend

avionics—electrical systems used on airplanes and spacecraft

blimps—types of airships

classified information— information that only top military people know

emblems—a person or thing used to represent something

flytime—how long an airplane can fly without stopping to refuel

ground-based sensors—computer systems on land that can find and locate ships and airplanes

hydrofoil—a fast boat that rises up out of the water when it reaches high speeds

icebreakers—large boats that cut through thick ice

Mach—a unit of measurement for speeds faster than the speed of sound

malfunction—when something does not work as it is supposed to

malnutrition—when a person's body doesn't get the right vitamins and nutrients

mothership—a ship or airplane that carries smaller ships or airplanes

NATO—the abbreviation for North Atlantic Treaty Organization, a coalition of 28 countries that help each other with defense

operational checks—all of the things people need to do to make sure everything is working on a boat or plane before it is deployed

ramjet—a type of jet engine where the air is sucked in and compressed by the forward motion of the airplane

range—the maximum distance ammunition can travel to reach its target; or the distance that a vehicle can travel without refueling

sophisticated—complex

supersonic—faster than the speed of sound

READ MORE

Leavitt, Amie Jane. *U.S. Navy by the Numbers*. Military by the Numbers. North Mankato, Minn.: Capstone Press, 2014.

Perritano, John and James Spears. *Everything Battles*. National Geographic Kids Everything. Washington, D.C.: National Geographic Kids, 2013.

Wesley, Jack. *Military Vehicles*. Scholastic Discover More Readers. New York: Scholastic, 2014.

INTERNET SITES

FactHound offers a safe, fun way to find Internet sites related to this book. All of the sites on FactHound have been researched by our staff.

Here's all you do:

Visit *www.facthound.com*

Type in this code: 9781515745266

INDEX

Mind Benders are published by Capstone,
1710 Roe Crest Drive, North Mankato, Minnesota 56003
www.mycapstone.com

Library of Congress Cataloging-in-Publication Data
Names: Meister, Cari, author.
Title: Totally amazing facts about military sea and air vehicles / by Cari Meister.
Description: North Mankato, Minnesota : Capstone Press, [2017] | Series: Mind
    benders | Includes bibliographical references and index. | Audience: Grades 4–6.
Identifiers: LCCN 2016019262 | ISBN 9781515745266 (library binding) |
    ISBN 9781515745280 (paperback) | ISBN 9781515745303 (ebook PDF)
Subjects: LCSH: Airplanes, Military—United States—Juvenile literature. |
Warships—United States—Juvenile literature.
Classification: LCC UG1243 .M444 2017 | DDC 623.74/6—dc23
LC record available at https://lccn.loc.gov/2016019262

Editor: Megan Atwood
Designer: Kyle Grenz
Media Researcher: Jo Miller
Production Specialist: Tori Abraham

Photo Credits

Alamy: INTERFOTO, 27, PF-(aircraft), 61, PF-(sdasm3), 28, Stocktrek Images/Daniele Faccioli, 31, War Archive, 18; AP Images: U.S. Army, 38; Gamma-Rapho via Getty Images: Reporters Associes, 63; Getty Images: Bettmann, 26, 37, 50, TASS, 80, The LIFE Picture Collection/Ralph Crane, 4; Glow Images: Deposit Photos, 66; NARA, 26-27 (background); NASA, 14, 15; Newscom: akg-images, 36, European Press Agency/Sergel_Supinsky, 41, Everett Collection, 7 (right), Heritage Images/Ann Ronan Picture Library, 16, Hilary Jane Morgan, 17 (left), Reuters/Andrew Innerarity, 29, Reuters/Robert Kolek, 40, Tass Photos/Zarembo Igor Itar, 104, Xinhua News Agency/Chen Rui, 23, ZUMA Press/EPN/Dong-Min Jang, 52 (F-15K), ZUMA Press/Keystone Pictures USA, 91, ZUMA Press/TASS, 97, Nova Development Corporation, 100-101 (flags); NY Daily News Archive via Getty Images/Joe Petrella, 39; Shutterstock: 13ree.design, 109 (bottom right), 3DMaestro, 67, admin_design, 53 (South Korea flag), advent, 51, Alfredo Cerra, 74, B Calkins, 78 (background), Brian Goff, 93, dedek, 3 (killer whale), Demeshko Alexandr, 65 (submarine), 102-103 (submarines), dreamnikon, 52 (F-15CJ/DJ), Elena Terletskaya, 77 (top), Everett Historical, 64, Gaulois_s, 94 (bottom), Getmilitaryphotos, 83, HedgehogVector, 105, Hurst Photo, 5 (bottom), Iakov Filimonov, 76, Ivan Kotliar, 86, Jacky Co, 55, Jane Kelly, 17 (right), konahinab, 56 (wings), KWJPHOTOART, cover (top left), LINE ICONS, 48 (top), Liudmyia Marykon, 47 (UFOs), lukpedclub, 46 (pancake), mariocigic, 107 (background), Marzolino, 77 (bottom), mavi, 73 (bottom), Milos Kontic, 22, momojung, 94 (top), MSPhotographic, 73 (top), Naci Yavuz, 7 (left), NEGOVURA, 109 (top left), Patrick Foto, back cover (bottom left), PILart, 108, shtiel, 19, Skalapendra, 46 (wings), SoRad, 25, StudioIcon, 72 (top), Svetlana Guteneva, 109 (top right), THPStock, 28 (background), Thumbelina, 3 (tank), tovovan, 57, Tsibii Lesia, 53 (USA, China, Japan, Vietnam, and Russia flags), Victor Brave, back cover (bottom left), Vladvm, 109 (bottom left), Volina, 79; U.S. Air Force photo by Master Sgt. Andy Dunaway, 10, Master Sgt. Kevin J. Gruenwald, 32, Osakabe Yasuo, 2, 3 (top), Senior Airman Brian Ferguson, 42, Senior Airman Chris Massey, 52 (F-22A), Staff Sgt. Aaron Allmon, cover (top right), 33, Staff Sgt. Bennie J. Davis III, 34, 35, Staff Sgt. Courtney Richardson, cover (bottom right), 106, Tech. Sgt. Justin D. Pyle, 43, Tech. Sgt. Robert J. Horstman, 8, Master Sgt. Greg Steele, 9; U.S. Army photo by Denise DeMonia, 20, Maj. Christopher Thomas, 44, Spc. Randis Monroe, 45, Staff Sgt. Bryanna Poulin, 21; U.S. Navy photo, cover (bottom left), Lt. Jan Shultis, 84, Mass Communication Specialist 1st Class Jeffrey Jay Price, 70, Mass Communication Specialist 2nd Class Brian Caracci, 12, Mass Communication Specialist 2nd Class Jillian Lotti, 24, Mass Communication Specialist 3rd Class Mark Andrew Hays, 75, OS2 John Bouvia, 68, PH3 Rodney W. Jones, 13, courtesy of Naval Sea Systems Command, 88; Wikimedia, 56, Alex Beltyukov, 52 (T-50), Azurri13579, 52 (SU-30MKV), Dmitriy Pichugin, 52 (SU-27SK), FOX 52, 100, GFDL, 6, Kaboldy, 60, NARA, 87, National Archives, 5 (top), National Archives, back cover (right), SSGT REYNALDO RAMON, USAF, 48 (bottom), SSGT REYNALDO RAMON, USAF, 49, U.S. Naval Historical Center, 72 (bottom), US Navy, 47, 58, XaHyMaH, 30

Design Elements by Capstone and Shutterstock

112